Executing Strategy

Pocket Mentor Series

The *Pocket Mentor* series offers immediate solutions to common challenges managers face on the job every day. Each book in the series is packed with handy tools, self-tests, and real-life examples to help you identify your strengths and weaknesses and hone critical skills. Whether you're at your desk, in a meeting, or on the road, these portable guides enable you to tackle the daily demands of your work with greater speed, savvy, and effectiveness.

Books in the series:

Executing
Strategy
Expert
Solutions to
Everyday Challenges

Harvard Business Press

Boston, Massachusetts

Executing Strategy.
     p. cm. — (Pocket mentor series)
  Includes bibliographical references.
  ISBN 978-1-4221-2889-3 (pbk.)
 1. Strategic planning.
  HD30.28.E957 2009
  658.4'012—dc22

                         2009010446

Contents

Mentor's Message: The Power of a Well-Executed Strategy

Most strategies (plans for producing specific business outcomes) fail to deliver their promised results—whether it's higher profitability, greater market share, better employee engagement, or some other desired benefit. Why such disappointment? The problem usually doesn't lie in the strategy planning process; it lies in the execution process—the steps taken to carry out the strategic plan. Even the most brilliant strategy is useless unless people throughout a unit or an organization can put the strategy into action.

This book introduces you to the strategy planning process, but then emphasizes the steps you can take as a manager to ensure that the strategy your company or unit has devised delivers as promised.

C. Davis Fogg, Mentor

Dave Fogg is a keynote speaker and strategic planning consultant who specializes in developing and implementing corporate strategic plans. He is a former General Manager of Johnston & Murphy and president of Bausch & Lomb's Consumer Products Divisions. He has taught strategic planning, strategic implementation, and general management courses at Vanderbilt, Columbia, Emory, MIT, Penn State, and the University of Wisconsin. He is the author of three books: *Diagnostic Marketing, Team-Based Strategic Planning,* and *Implementing Your Strategic Plan.* He has also published a series of strategic manuals. *Leading Your Organization Through Strategic and Departmental Planning* provides step-by-step instructions on how to conduct and facilitate the entire planning process.

Executing Strategy: The Basics

The Role of Strategy

Everyone seems to recognize how important strategy is to a company. Yet there is considerable debate on just what strategy is and how to create and execute it—how to put it into action. The sections below address these gaps.

What is strategy?

This book views strategy as a process that spurs major change so that an organization can achieve outstanding results. Strategy is about understanding what you do, looking out over the long-term future to determine what you want to become, and—most important—focusing on how you plan to get there.

For example, consider a company that makes video games. Its primary business is to entertain people. As the company looks into the future, it might determine that one of its long-term priorities is to have its brand name known throughout the world. The company's strategy would therefore focus on how the organization plans to grow its business and brand, and how it intends to enter global markets over the coming years.

Strategy can be viewed as a blend of art and science. It is an art in that strategy requires creative thought, an ability to identify alternative future states, and strong communication skills to inspire and engage those who will implement the strategy. It is a science in that it requires managers to collect and analyze information that they can then turn into action.

Why is strategy important?

It's not enough for a company to develop a successful product or service. Without a strategy, an organization is rudderless—and vulnerable to business changes as well as competitive threats. A sound strategy, skillfully carried out, fosters significant shifts in the way a company does business, and these shifts distinguish a company from its competitors. By guiding a company's ongoing evolution, strategy provides the necessary information and direction for managers to define their work—and help their organization remain competitive.

> *Every moment spent planning saves three or four in execution.*
> —Crawford Greenwalt

How is strategy formulated?

Broadly speaking, strategy is achieved through two fundamental processes: planning and execution. Many companies involve both senior management and business units in the strategic planning processes. Units are involved because they house tremendous knowledge about an organization and can make informed recommendations about what a company should be doing and where it should be going. Furthermore, when units are included in planning, they are more likely to support and carry out the plans that are created.

In short, units are the execution centers of an organization. They have the leadership, people, skills, and money needed to carry out a strategic plan. Without their support, even a brilliant strategy will go nowhere.

Organizations that fail to include units when planning strategy typically produce results inferior to those that do. By undertaking the planning process together, senior management and units ensure that a company's strategies—corporate and unit—are tightly aligned and that successful execution can follow.

This book's focus

This book looks briefly at how companies undertake the strategic planning process and then examines in more detail how strategy is executed within an organization. We'll approach the topic of strategy execution through the eyes of a manager or an individual within a unit—not from the perspective of senior management.

A note about terminology

Each company plans and executes strategy in its own unique way. As a result, the way the processes unfold and the terms associated with these processes vary from company to company. This book examines the key elements of the strategic planning and execution processes and defines terms broadly to reach as many people as possible.

The Strategic Plan: Four Key Elements

Before discussing the strategic planning process, it's helpful to understand the elements of a strategic plan—the outgrowth of the planning process. While strategic plans vary, they generally contain the following components:

- Direction statement

- Strategic objectives

- Priority issues

- Action plans

Organizations may use different terms for these components and may differ in how they describe them. However, most organizations provide an array of information about their strategy and, in broad terms, explain how they plan to achieve it.

Direction statement

One does not plan and then try to make circumstances fit those plans.
One tries to make plans fit the circumstances.
—George S. Patton Jr.

A direction statement acts as a guide for an organization's actions and thinking. While this statement can be captured in different formats—ranging from a succinct one- or two-page document to a variety of informal communications—it usually provides the following information about an organization:

- **Mission:** the organization's purpose

- **Vision:** the organization's deeply desired future

- **Business definition:** the firm's existing and envisioned products, services, geographic distribution, technology, customers, and markets

- **Competitive advantages:** customer needs that the organization plans to meet better than competitors do

- **Core competencies:** the tangible assets (e.g., manufacturing plants) and intangible ones (such as R&D prowess) the company will leverage to gain competitive advantage

- **Values:** the driving beliefs that define a company's culture (e.g., innovation) and that support the organization's future competitive advantage

Strategic objectives

Strategic objectives allow a company to measure how it is performing in key result areas (KRAs)—those areas where the company must achieve superior results to execute its long-term strategy. Key result areas often come directly from a company's direction statement.

For example, if a company's vision is global expansion, then it will want to measure success in that area. Areas for which a

?

How Will Information Technology Contribute?

J AKE HAS RECENTLY become a manager of an information technology (IT) group. During the strategic planning process, senior management has identified the company's cost structure as a weakness that needs to be addressed for the company to remain competitive. Senior management has established a corresponding strategic objective: "Reduce costs 5 percent annually throughout the organization for the next three years."

As part of strategic planning, senior management has asked the company's units to find ways to address this cost-structure problem and propose other issues that need attention. Jake is wondering how best to begin complying with this request.

What would YOU do? The mentor will suggest a solution in *What You COULD Do*.

company might set strategic objectives are market position, customer loyalty, quality, service, innovation, and human capital.

Management must decide how it will measure success in the KRAs and then set objectives for those measures. For instance, if customer loyalty is a KRA, it might be measured by a customer satisfaction index. The corresponding objective might be "Raise the customer satisfaction index from 89 to 96 in the next three years."

Priority issues

Priority issues are a company's primary instruments of action. These are the key issues that surface during the strategic planning process—for example, a weakness to be addressed or an opportunity to be seized.

Priority issues typically relate to competitive concerns—the products and services a company needs to create to add value for its customers, the internal process changes needed to support a company's strategy, and the skills and resources needed to create new value and enhance business processes. Common priority issues are costs, service, new markets and products, geographic expansion, acquisitions, divestitures, organizational structure, core competencies and processes, new technologies, training and development, and information systems.

The successful implementation of a company's strategy hinges on turning priority issues into high-level action plans and delegating those plans to units or cross-functional teams. To illustrate, a company might determine that market share is a priority issue and set an objective of increasing it by 10 percent in the next three years. A marketing unit might be asked to develop action plans to determine how to "acquire competitors that will add at least 5 percent in niches in which the company is now weak."

Action plans

Priority issues are translated into high-level action plans for strategic initiatives (also known as projects or programs). Action plans briefly describe the specific steps the company needs to take to accomplish its priority issues—and thereby achieve its objectives. A single priority issue might spawn two or three action plans. For example, if cost is a priority issue, it may yield three action plans: a plan for overhead costs, one for operating costs, and another for selling and marketing costs.

A high-level action plan for a strategic initiative typically includes descriptions of these elements:

- The priority issue and why it's important
- Objectives expressed in specific metrics and time frames
- Key steps involved in achieving the priority issue
- Resources required
- Interlocking requirements involving other units
- Anticipated cost and gain

An organization's strategic plan results from the strategic planning process.

What You COULD Do

Remember Jake's concern about how to support senior management's top priority issues?

Here's what the mentor suggests:

The first step is for Jake and his group to analyze external and internal information—for example, market segmentation (external) and core processes (internal). He and his team should then conduct a *SWOT analysis*, that is, an evaluation of his group's strengths, weaknesses, opportunities, and threats. From these analyses, priority issues will emerge—in addition to the one that has been already delegated by senior management. Jake and his group will narrow the list of priority issues down to three or four and submit them to senior management for review. Once these are approved, Jake and his team will need to create high-level action plans that support each of the priority issues.

The Strategic
Planning Process:
Five Steps

The strategic planning process is the primary vehicle for achieving strategic alignment across an organization and ensuring the effective execution of a company's strategy. The result of the planning process is a strategic plan.

The strategic planning process typically begins with extensive research and analysis that helps senior management zero in on the top three or four priority issues that the company needs to tackle to be successful in the long term. For each priority issue, management asks units and teams to create high-level action plans. Once these action plans are developed, the company's high-level strategic objectives and direction statement are further clarified.

Strategic planning consists of five steps:

1. Analyze external and internal factors.

2. Perform SWOT (strengths, weaknesses, opportunities, and threats) analyses.

3. Draft priority issues.

4. Develop high-level action plans.

5. Finalize the plan.

While this process may seem linear and straightforward, strategic planning is anything but. It's an iterative process that takes time and requires a series of back-and-forth communications between senior management and units, whereby all parties examine, discuss, and refine the plan. As a result, various planning streams often happen in parallel.

> *I have always found that plans are useless, but planning is indispensable.*
> —Dwight D. Eisenhower

How does the strategic planning process begin for a unit? It varies from company to company. Often, a unit will begin with certain strategic objectives and priority issues that have already been determined and delegated by senior management. For example, senior management might have a priority that focuses on global markets and may delegate this issue to the appropriate units. A unit that receives this priority will then factor it into its strategic planning. In other cases, a unit will embark on the planning process without any predetermined priority issues.

Let's look more closely now at each step in the planning process.

Step 1: Analyze external and internal factors

A unit begins its planning process with research and analysis. It analyzes factors such as trends and forces—both external and internal to the organization—and assesses their future impact on the unit. *Trends* typically describe a pattern of behavior and occur over long periods, while *forces* describe abrupt or disruptive changes that tend to occur more quickly.

Considering both external and internal factors is essential—because they clarify the business world in which the unit operates, enabling the unit to better envision its desired future. Analyzing external factors surfaces potential opportunities and threats, while analyzing internal factors surfaces strengths and weaknesses.

External trends and forces include the following:

- **Market:** developments in the marketplace in areas such as segmentation, customer needs, and competitive advantage

- **Technology:** electronic commerce and other developments related to technology

- **Legislation:** new laws, legislative control, regulations, and government intervention

- **Partnerships:** alliances with outside firms, vendors, and business associates

- **Culture:** varying workforce ethics for different people

Analyzing market segmentation and customer needs is especially important in developing a strategic plan. For this analysis, a unit researches market segments—groups of customers within a broad market and whose needs and wants are similar—and asks questions such as these: How are markets segmented now—and how might they be segmented in the long term? What segments should the company target? What gaps must be filled to beat the competition?

Internal trends and forces include the following:

- **Core competencies:** the status of the company's assets, expertise, and skills needed to yield superior performance

- **Core processes:** the status of the processes needed to do business and deliver competitive advantage

- **Financial measures:** spending history, baseline forecasts, portfolio analysis, return on assets

- **Key result areas:** the history of the company's performance in areas such as innovation, customer satisfaction, employee retention, and operating results

- **Management:** how the company determines accountability, delegates decision making, uses teams, and rewards performance

- **Organizational culture:** the values, attitudes, and shared beliefs of the organization's employees

Step 2: Perform SWOT analyses

Analyzing external and internal factors informs the next step in the process, a SWOT analysis—identifying the company's or unit's strengths, weaknesses, opportunities, and threats.

- **Strengths:** capabilities that enable your company or unit to perform well and that need to be leveraged

- **Weaknesses:** characteristics that prohibit your company or unit from performing well and that must be addressed

- **Opportunities:** trends, forces, events, and ideas that your company or unit can capitalize on

- **Threats:** possible events or forces, outside of your control, that your company or unit needs to plan for or decide how to mitigate

Steps for conducting a SWOT analysis

1. **Select an individual to facilitate the SWOT analysis.**
2. **Brainstorm a company or unit's strengths.** Go around the room and solicit ideas from participants. Areas of strength for a company or unit include leadership abilities, decision-making abilities, innovation, productivity, quality, service, efficiency, technological processes, and so forth. Record all suggestions on a flip chart. Avoid duplicate entries. Make it clear that some issues may appear on more than one list. For example, a company or unit may have a strength in an area such as customer service, but may have a weakness or deficiency in that area as well. At this point, the goal is to capture as many ideas on the flip charts as possible. Evaluating the strengths will take place later.
3. **Consolidate ideas.** Post all flip charts pages on a wall. While every effort may have been taken to avoid duplicate entries, some ideas will overlap. Consolidate duplicate points by asking the group which items can be combined under the same subject. Resist the temptation to overconsolidate—that is, avoid lumping lots of ideas under one subject. Often, this results in a lack of focus.
4. **Clarify ideas.** Go down the consolidated list item by item, and clarify any items that participants have questions about. It's helpful to reiterate the meaning of each item before discussing it. Stick to defining strengths. Restrain the team from talking about solutions at this point in the process.
5. **Identify the top three strengths.** Sometimes, the top three strengths are obvious and no vote is necessary. In that case, simply test for consensus. Otherwise, give participants a few

minutes to pick their top issues individually. Allow each team member to cast three to five votes (three if the list of issues is ten items or fewer, five if it is long). Identify the top three items. If there are ties or the first vote is inconclusive, discuss the highly rated items from the first vote, and vote again.

6. **Summarize strengths.** Once the top three strengths are selected, summarize them on a single flip-chart page.

7. **Repeat steps 2–6 for weaknesses.** Similar to strengths, areas of weakness for a company or unit include leadership abilities, decision-making abilities, innovation, productivity, quality, service, efficiency, technological processes, and so forth.

8. **Repeat steps 2–6 for opportunities.** Areas of opportunities include emerging markets, further market penetration, new technologies, new products or services, geographic expansion, cost reduction, and so forth.

9. **Repeat steps 2–6 for threats.** Areas of threat include the entrance of a new competitor, legislation or regulations that will increase costs or eliminate a product, a declining product or market, and so forth.

A unit may conduct two SWOT analyses—one focused on the company and another on the unit. The goal is to help your company or unit identify opportunities that it must take advantage of to reach its mission or vision in five to ten years. SWOT analyses are also important because they identify possible threats that may prevent a company or unit from being successful. Through brainstorming and intensive debate, a number of priority issues begin to emerge.

Step 3: Draft priority issues

After analyzing trends and forces and conducting SWOT analyses, unit leaders will have gathered a wealth of information about the company and their unit. The next step is to draft priority issues— broad areas in which unit leaders think the company and unit should focus efforts for the long term.

In most cases, priority issues emerge directly from the SWOT analyses. A priority issue is a strength to be bolstered, a critical weakness to be fixed, an opportunity to be capitalized on, or a threat to be mitigated. Leaders evaluate priority issues and select a few—those that have the most positive impact on the long-term direction of the company or unit.

For example, after conducting a SWOT analysis for the company, a unit manager identified an opportunity to expand the unit's products into developing countries and thus drafted a priority issue on entering new markets. Another manager, after conducting a SWOT analysis for her unit, learned that the unit was weak in innovation. This manager therefore made innovation a priority to be addressed going forward.

After lengthy discussion and debate, unit leaders identify the top three or four priority issues and present them to senior management for review. Senior management reviews the priority issues that have been submitted by all the units in addition to the priority issues that it has generated itself. Reviewing the priority issues takes time and requires extensive back-and-forth between senior management and unit leaders.

Using specific criteria that are defined up front, senior managers eventually narrow down the list of priority issues and select

Steps for determining priority issues

1. **Review the results of the SWOT analysis.** At the end of the SWOT analysis, you will have generated four summary lists—one each for strengths, weaknesses, opportunities, and threats. On each of these lists, you will have identified the top three items for each category. Post these summary lists on a wall for everyone to review.

2. **Identify priority issues from the SWOT analysis.** Priority issues typically emerge from the SWOT analysis. They are strengths to be bolstered, weaknesses to be corrected, opportunities to be capitalized on, and threats to be avoided. Priority issues generally meet one or more of the following criteria: they have long-term and major positive financial impact; they address a fleeting window of opportunity (e.g., a developing new market or available acquisitions); or they are critical in correcting any structural weaknesses.

3. **Compile priority issues.** Ask participants to select their top three priority issues from the SWOT summary lists, giving them sufficient time to scan the list and write down their choices. Go around the room, asking each person to name his or her highest priority issue (from the top three) without repeating issues already mentioned. Continue to solicit issues until no more are forthcoming.

4. **Elicit discussion.** Ensure that each proposed priority issue is clear. Discuss the reason for proposing it, the advantage of addressing it, and the disadvantage of not addressing it. Priority issues are typically broad areas that a company or unit wants

to focus on. Examples include cost, profitability, innovation, and service. Be wary of priority issues that are too narrow. An item as narrow as "manufacturing reject rate and cost" may be of minor strategic importance. The bigger issue might be overall manufacturing cost structure.

5. **Address overlooked priority issues.** Sometimes priority issues are overlooked during this process. Ask participants to suggest any obvious omissions. For example, a team of retailers arrived at a list of five priority issues, none of which addressed the significant weakness of an uncompetitive cost structure. Once pointed out, this became their highest priority for the next several years.

6. **Vote on priority issues.** Ask participants to cast three votes on the list of remaining priority-issue candidates. Identify the three to five priority issues that earn the most votes. As a final step, record why participants felt that these issues were important.

---

the three or four key issues the company will pursue. They delegate those priority issues to the appropriate units or to cross-functional teams for execution.

Step 4: Develop high-level action plans

Once the priority issues have been approved and delegated to the appropriate units for implementation, the units or teams then create high-level action plans that briefly detail the objectives, tasks, and other requirements for carrying out a strategic initiative. Each priority issue typically generates two to three action plans. For example, if customer retention is a priority, it may lead to two action plans: one for improving customer service and another for developing a customer loyalty program.

Once a unit has developed its action plans, the unit leaders send the plans to senior management for review and discussion. If revisions are necessary, senior management will ask the units to refine their action plans. At a resource-allocation meeting, the refined action plans are approved, any cross-functional teams are designated, and senior management allocates the resources required to carry out the plans. Senior management's allocation of resources is critical in aligning units' actions behind the corporate strategy.

Step 5: Finalize the plan

The final step in the process is to put the finishing touches on the plan. Senior management typically writes a corporate direction statement (if one doesn't already exist) and clarifies the high-level objectives that summarize the organization's overarching initiatives. At this point, units might also choose to draft a direction statement and high-level objectives to summarize their own efforts over the long term. During the planning process, units may have identified priority issues and tasks at the unit level; these priorities will strategically and structurally move the unit toward fulfilling its own mission and vision.

Once a strategic plan is in place, managers will review, assess, and adjust the plan on an ongoing basis as circumstances change.

The key priority issues addressed in a strategic plan grow out of a careful examination of external and internal factors. If these factors remain constant, the plan is likely to need only minor adjustments. But if the factors change dramatically, then the plan will need to be reevaluated and changed.

Your Strategic-Initiative Action Plan

T he successful execution of strategy hinges on turning priority issues into action plans for strategic initiatives *and* then carrying out those action plans at the unit level. It's at this point that strategic planning and execution overlap.

An action plan for a strategic initiative contains the long-term objectives and the broad steps required to carry out that initiative. Such a high-level action plan will spawn many, more detailed action plans. A unit's annual planning process will probably involve integrating into the unit's annual goals the action plans that support strategic initiatives.

Components of the action plan

A strategic-initiative action plan typically contains the following information:

- **Priority issue:** a description of the broad area that the unit or team plans to focus on, and why it's important.

- **Objectives and metrics:** the intermediate- and long-term objectives (one, two, and three years ahead) of the strategic initiative. Objectives allow your unit to measure how it's performing. To determine your unit's objectives, you must decide on what metrics you will use to measure success. For example, if your unit puts a priority on entering new markets, it might have the following objective and corresponding metric: "Increase market penetration by 10 percent annually for the next five years in Latin American countries."

- **Steps:** the tasks that answer the *who*, *what*, and *when* involved in carrying out the initiative. Steps outline the four to five high-level tasks that need to be completed and that typically contain short-term objectives, measured in quarters or months. Eventually, action plans that are more detailed will be created for each individual step and will be owned by the people executing them.

- **Resources:** the required resources—people, money, technologies, and so forth—for carrying out the initiative.

- **Interlocks:** the required cross-functional collaborations needed to execute the initiative.

- **Impact estimate:** the anticipated cost and revenue potential of the project.

A sample action plan

Here's what a simplified, high-level action plan for a manufacturing unit in an electronics company might look like:

- **Unit:** Manufacturing.

- **Priority issue:** Long-range capacity.
  - **Description:** Design and build new facilities that will increase manufacturing's ability to produce higher unit volume at lower cost.

- **Strategic importance:** Our current capacity will not allow us to meet market demand or achieve our strategic objective of increasing market share.

- **Objectives and metrics:** Develop long-range manufacturing facilities that will meet forecast demand from 2010 to 2017; accommodate testing and manufacture of new products; and achieve dramatic improvement in quality, cost, and customer service.

  - **Year 1:** Complete the design phase and begin construction by year-end.

  - **Year 2:** Complete construction and start production by year-end.

  - **Year 3:** Achieve initial running rate of 177 million units per year at a cost of $0.325 per unit.

- **Steps:** (simplified for purposes of illustration)

Year 1

What	Who	When
Establish design specifications	Manufacturing team; engineering leads	January 2010
Approve specs	Senior management	February 2010
Flow-chart and system design; costing	Manufacturing team; engineering and finance lead	June 2010
Detailed drawings for bid purposes; costing	Manufacturing team; engineering and finance lead	August 2010
Approval	Senior management	August 2010

| Bids | Purchasing and construction | October 2010 |
| Construction starts | Construction team from manufacturing and facilities takes over | November 2010 |

- **Resources:** Need to hire one full-time construction manager, two plant managers from groundbreaking on, and three assistants to support these managers.

- **Interlocks:** (simplified for purposes of illustration)

Manufacturing unit works with	To	Start when
Construction unit	Manage entire construction process	January 1, 2010
Legal	Handle all licenses, liability assessment, and insurance	March 1, 2010
Customers	Form customer service committee to design order-entry shipment systems	May 1, 2010

- **Impact estimate:**

Cost:	Expense capital = $125M			
	Other capital = $125M			
	Equipment = $250M			
	Total investment = $500M			

Revenue: (new plant)		Yr 1	Yr 3	Yr 5
	Price/unit	$0.425	$0.400	$0.350
	Cost/unit	$0.325	$0.270	$0.180
	Units	177M	525M	700M
	Revenue	$75M	$210M	$500M

Defining Objectives
and Metrics

While your company identifies overarching long-term, strategic objectives, your unit may have determined some strategic objectives of its own. Further, an action plan for a strategic initiative typically has longer-term objectives (e.g., for years 1, 2, and 3), with shorter-term objectives contained within the action plan steps.

For example, a company might have a mission to become known as number one in customer service in its industry—with a strategic objective of raising its customer service index by eight points over the next two years. Senior management might delegate this strategic objective to the customer service group while also declaring that service is the entire company's top priority. During the strategic planning process, marketing might then come up with a unit priority issue of customer loyalty, while sales focuses on customer retention as a unit priority. The action plans of these different initiatives might have a common objective of completing a new customer database by the end of year 1. The action plan for the sales unit's customer retention initiative might have another objective of increasing customer retention by 20 percent by the end of year 3. Further, as a result of the planning process, the company might update its corporate strategy to include the area of customer retention.

In effect, the company, its units, and its strategic initiatives have a number of cascading and related objectives, with metrics tailored to the units' unique business processes.

How do you effectively define objectives and measure performance? You identify key result areas, determine measures for success, and write objectives. We'll look at each of these below.

Identifying key result areas

Senior management often determines the overarching key result areas (KRAs) by which a company's and a unit's overall success will be measured. Units typically have from four to six KRAs by which they are measured. Units may also determine KRAs of their own.

Different functions are measured in different ways. Consider the following examples of some KRAs that might be measured for three units:

KRAs for different units

Marketing unit	Manufacturing unit	Human resources unit
• Sales • Market penetration • New products • Pricing • Distribution	• Unit volume • Cost • Efficiency • Quality • Process • Innovation	• Training • Recruitment • Compliance • Compensation/wages • Leadership

Determining measures for success

If you can't measure it, you can't manage it.

—Peter F. Drucker

Once a unit's KRAs are determined, leaders then define how success will be measured. Through those metrics, unit objectives can be defined. For example, for a manufacturing unit, two KRAs and their corresponding metrics and objectives might be as follows:

Key result area	Metric	Objectives
Cost	Cost per unit	• By end of year 1, cost per unit will be $79.50 • By end of year 2, cost per unit will be $71.00
	Units per employee per year	• By end of year 1, units per employee per year will be 15,000 • By end of year 2, units per employee per year will be 24,000
Safety	Work-hours lost per year	• By end of year 1, work-hours lost per year will be 25 • By end of year 2, work-hours lost per year will be 10
	Plant safety index	• By end of year 1, plant safety index will be 94 • By end of year 2, plant safety index will be 96

Whatever performance measurement system your company or unit uses, you need to have a clear system for measuring progress and evaluating performance. The right objectives and metrics will help.

Writing objectives

When writing objectives, make sure they are SMART—specific, measurable, achievable, realistic, and time-bound. Here are examples of SMART and not-so-SMART objectives:

SMART objective	Not-so-SMART objective
In the next three years, add twenty new systems engineers who are capable of handling the new advanced programming language—year 1, add two new people; year 2, add nine new people; and year 3, add nine new people.	Add new systems engineers who are capable of handling the new advanced programming language. [Objective is not specific, measurable, or time-bound.]
Raise sales 10 percent annually over the next three years.	Improve sales over the next year. [Not specific or measurable.]
Reduce average duration of customer service phone calls by 30 percent over the next two years.	Reduce average duration of customer service phone calls by 50 percent over the next year. [Not likely to be achievable or realistic.]

Steps for identifying objectives

1. **Define key results areas (KRAs).** Make sure participants understand that KRAs are areas of business activity in which a unit must excel in order to meet customer needs, beat competition, and exceed stakeholder expectations. Typical KRAs include cost, customer service, innovation, new products, and quality. Most units have between four and six KRAs.

2. **Solicit KRA ideas and associated measures.** Go around the room, and solicit KRA ideas from participants. Record all suggestions on a flip chart. Allow only comments that seek clarification, not those that seek to critique an idea. For each proposed KRA, list the measurements for success. For example, if a unit identifies customer satisfaction as a KRA, the group

might measure this by "number of complaints in a year" and "number of products returned versus ordered in a year."

3. **Through voting, determine the four to six KRAs and their corresponding measures that your unit will focus on.**

4. **Create objectives.** For each KRA, using the measures that have been defined, draft specific long-term objectives. For example, if customer satisfaction is a KRA and "number of complaints in a year" is a measurement for success, a unit might draft this objective: "Reduce the number of complaints by 30 percent in 2012."

Identifying the
Resources Needed

Strategic-initiative action plans outline the resources that will be required for an initiative to be carried out. Resources include much more than just money and can take various forms, including these:

- People
- Technologies
- Office space
- Systems
- Support from other departments
- Vendors and strategic partners
- Time
- Training

Below, we examine ways to estimate your resource needs over the long term.

Estimating your resource needs

Be ruthless in selecting superlative people for your future needs.

—Meriwether Lewis

Managers often make the mistake of not taking enough time to assess and adequately estimate their resource needs. If they overlook this step or take shortcuts, they risk failing to execute their action plans successfully. Here are some questions you might ask when assessing your resource needs:

- How will the strategic initiative affect my group's ongoing day-to-day work?

- Can our existing resources cover the strategic-initiative action plans in addition to business as usual?

- If not, what additional resources will my unit need?

- What new skills will people need if they are to carry out a strategic initiative?

- What training will be required? At what cost?

- What new systems or technology will be required to support the initiative? At what cost?

Thinking long term

As you think about the resources your unit needs, remember to look beyond just what the group needs today, and consider what it might need in the coming years. By forecasting skills and competencies that your group will need in the future and by hiring for "tomorrow," you can keep pace with the market and build a competitive advantage.

For example, suppose your company's long-term strategy calls for leveraging an up-and-coming technology—and designing new products using that technology. You may anticipate needing team members skilled in the technology a year down the road. In this case, you might train some employees in that technology *now* to lay the foundation for handling work that will come later.

Planning ahead, thinking strategically, and leveraging current resources are key management skills in today's world of constrained resources. Your goal is to end up with the right people and skills you need—by the time you need them.

Clarifying
Interlocks

Most units don't work in isolation to execute their strategy. They need to collaborate with others—inside and outside the company—to put their strategic plans into action. The following sections shed light on how to manage these "interlocks."

The need for cross-functional collaboration

Interlocks, or cross-functional collaborations, lead to two types of exchanges. Sometimes, your unit will need to *receive* work from other units so that you can implement your action plans. Other times, your unit will need to *give* work to other units so that they can carry out their own action plans. Typically, several groups will need to collaborate to carry out a strategic initiative, and the interlocks can be substantial.

Consider this example: Your company may have a priority issue that focuses on market share, with an objective of growing its market share by 30 percent over the next five years. This corporate priority issue and objective will probably have an impact on many (if not all) units in the company. In developing action plans, units throughout the organization may find that they need to collaborate with other units to implement their plans. For example:

If your unit is ...	You might need ...	For help in ...
Sales	Human resources	Designing a series of courses on effective cross-selling
Marketing	Information technology	Building a customer database that distinguishes market segments
Product development	Finance	Clarifying new business models

When collaboration across groups becomes extensive, companies often form cross-functional teams comprising representatives from each unit that has interlocking obligations.

Using the above example, a company may decide that the objective necessitates creating a cross-functional team. In this case, the team might be led by someone from the marketing unit and include others from product development, sales, and information technology. As needed, the team might pull in members from finance and human resources.

When cross-functional teams are created, they typically develop a charter that outlines the team's roles, responsibilities, key milestones, deliverables, and decision-making processes.

The challenge of coordinating across groups

Many managers find intergroup coordination incredibly challenging. Why? It requires them to assist, and to obtain assistance from, people over whom they have no formal authority. Thus, when

Tips for navigating interlocks

- Determine any required cross-functional collaboration that will be needed to carry out strategic initiatives, and include those "interlocking" requirements within the associated action plans.

- Get clear approval for any interlocks from senior management. This is part of strategic planning.

- When the interlocks for carrying out a strategic initiative are substantial, consider creating a formal cross-functional team and charging it with carrying out the initiative.

- If you will need help from another group, notify this group as early as you can about your needs, and set expectations up front. Involve the group in determining the specific interlocks needed, and include those interlocks in your action plans. Later, as the time approaches when the agreed-upon help will be needed, remind the group about the upcoming interlocks. Be sure to give the group plenty of notice.

- If an agreement on interlocks cannot be reached, identify this as an area of high risk in your action plan. Failure to agree on interlocks is a source of potential conflict within organizations—and a common cause of the derailment of an initiative.

- Document all your interlock needs, expectations, and agreements, and document any agreed-upon changes to those interlocks.

creating high-level action plans, be sure to discuss and negotiate interlock requirements early so you can align all the varied resources you'll need to successfully carry out your unit's plans.

To ensure accountability, document all interlock needs, expectations, and obligations—as well as any changes in the interlocks. If an interlock agreement cannot be reached, identify it as an area of high risk in the action plan.

Failure to agree on interlock arrangements can spawn intense conflict between groups in organizations—especially during times of tight resources. If any such conflicts arise during implementation of one of your action plans, raise these issues and resolve them immediately to keep the plan on course.

Keeping Your
Action Plan
on Course

trategic alignment across a company is achieved through the planning process—including delegating priority issues, approving strategic-initiative action plans, and allocating resources. To ensure that the execution of an organization's strategy remains on course, senior managers and unit leaders must constantly review and assess progress. Let's now look at ways to do that.

Reviewing progress

You can track progress, and thus ensure alignment, through these practices:

- **Check in informally.** Stay close to the implementation action, and proactively uncover any hurdles by asking questions such as "Are people getting the resources they need? What is blocking progress? Are you getting timely responses to any issues raised?"

- **Report regularly.** Require weekly or monthly reports on the status of action plans. Project Web sites or online team rooms can be useful for this—giving everyone access to the information and making progress visible to all.

- **Conduct quarterly reviews.** Quarterly reviews are an important tool for assessing progress and checking alignment. Typically, units or teams submit one- to two-page reports to senior management for each of the action plans they are implementing. These reports explain what the unit has accomplished, what the unit said it would accomplish but hasn't, key problems that need resolution, decisions or resources the unit needs from senior management, and performance to objectives, when relevant.

Understanding the causes of misalignment

Even the most carefully thought-out action plans can fall victim to misalignment or become derailed. Whatever the cause, misalignment and derailment are key issues that need to be aired and addressed during quarterly reviews. Misalignment and derailment can happen for various reasons:

- **Plans are expanded.** During the execution of action plans, a project may increase in scope. For example, a product development group might decide to add features to a new offering or to develop additional add-on products. Spending time on additional features and products then cuts into the resources intended to carry out the original plan.

- **Plans are trimmed.** Conversely, during the execution of action plans, a project may be cut back. This might be done to reduce costs or speed up implementation. While such measures might save money and time, they may also cause an action plan to fall short of achieving its original objectives.

- **Resources are inadequate.** Because of day-to-day responsibilities, people may not be given adequate time to work on

What Would YOU Do?

Tuning In to Strategy Execution

J ENNA MANAGES A MARKETING GROUP at Views, a wholesaler that distributes movie DVDs to retail stores. Many consumers, however, have begun buying and downloading movies from the Web instead of buying DVDs in retail stores. Consequently, retail stores have begun questioning how much value "expensive middleman" distributors, such as Views, really add. Senior management has defined an overarching strategic objective: "Add more value for these core customers—retail stores—by helping them attract more DVD buyers."

With input from Jenna's group and others, senior management decides its top priorities are pricing and marketing. Specifically, it is interested in decreasing the cost of DVDs and helping its retail-store customers with promotions. The groups are asked to develop action plans for these strategic initiatives.

Jenna's group develops two high-level action plans: (1) conducting market research on consumers who buy from the retail stores and (2) developing strong promotional campaigns for the stores. As the team members develop their market research action plan, they recognize that they will need help from the IT group to build a database to collect their retail-store customer and consumer data. Jenna knows that IT is overloaded with ongoing requests from other groups. She wonders how to secure the resources she'll need from IT.

What would YOU do? The mentor will suggest a solution in *What You COULD Do.*

---

strategic initiatives. This may stem from inaccurate resource estimates, an increase in project scope, or competing priorities. Or it may be that everyone just takes on too much, and resources are strained.

- **Interlocks change.** A group that your unit depends on for a deliverable or collaboration may alter its own plans and therefore not be able to fulfill its obligations to your unit. In many cases, this happens when another group's manager has failed to free up the necessary resources. Sometimes, interlocks are forgotten, or no one has informed another group in advance that its help will be needed. The cascading effect may make it difficult for your unit to meet its commitments and objectives.

- **Work processes change.** The way a task is being handled (e.g., getting employees to sign up for and complete a needed training program) might not be generating the desired results, so your unit needs to change a work process. This change may require additional funding and time that wasn't budgeted in the original plan.

- **Original estimates are inaccurate.** Your unit's original estimates for the time, effort, and costs needed to carry out an initiative turn out to be different from the realities. Estimates are often *lower* than the actual costs.

- **Politics interfere with progress.** A project may run into "political blockage"—people who didn't buy into a priority issue fail to carry out their obligations, causing delays and complications.

Anticipating misalignment

In executing any action plan, you will most likely face some degree of misalignment. After all, it's impossible to foresee with absolute certainty what resources every aspect of a project will require. Often, only by putting a plan into action can you get the most accurate sense of the resources you'll need. And when valuable new information is received, you need to be able to learn from it. For that reason, many managers build flexibility into their plans to allow for some surprises.

This often takes the form of contingency planning. For instance, for an initiative centering on a new training program, the manager in charge develops a plan for what he or she will do if the desired trainers are unavailable.

Tips for managing alignment

- Accept that changes to your strategic initiatives are inevitable.
- Be clear about who has final approval of changes. Establish a checks-and-balances system by ensuring that those who *propose* changes are not those who *approve* them.
- Whenever anyone suggests a change to an action plan, ask yourself, "Does this proposed change support our corporate strategy and priority issues?" If the suggested change doesn't support the corporate strategy, consider setting the idea aside and addressing it in the future.
- Clearly define all the ramifications—for both the unit and the company in general—of accepting and implementing a change to your action plans. Consider how the change will affect your deadlines, the overall costs, and the team members' workloads.
- If a proposed change requires further funding, additional people, or an extension of time not included in your original action plans, determine where those extra resources will come from. You may be able to redirect existing resources within your group without causing too much disruption to the rest of your plans. Or, such a change may require lobbying senior management for additional resources.

What You COULD Do

> Remember Jenna's worry about how she's going to secure IT resources?

Here's what the mentor suggests:

An important part of a high-level action plan is defining any dependencies on, and resources needed from, other groups—these interdependencies are sometimes called *interlocks*. Part of the planning process is establishing up front how groups will need to work together to achieve their strategic objectives. Senior management needs to allocate the available resources across strategic initiatives. Establishing interlocking dependencies and planning for them is a vital step in planning.

For these reasons, Jenna needs to meet with the head of IT as soon as possible to negotiate the resources she'll need from IT to carry out her group's initiative. By agreeing on and documenting this interlock in specific terms, she can be more confident that the IT manager will follow through on the promised assistance.

Establishing Accountability

O nce senior management has approved units' high-level action plans and allocated the required resources, the units are ready to begin executing their strategic initiatives. The first step is to establish accountability for the different tasks broadly outlined in the plan. Here are some suggestions for doing so.

Identifying responsibilities

Managers need to determine who will be responsible for the overall strategic action plan and, in turn, who will "own," or be responsible for, each of the different steps required to execute the plan. For example, suppose your unit has a priority issue that focuses on innovation and has created an objective of developing five new products over the next three years. The action plan will contain the four or five critical steps required to achieve that objective and, hence, that priority issue. The steps, simplified for purposes of illustration, might look something like this:

Year 1

What	Who	When
Conduct market research to assess customer needs	Marketing team	January 2010
Synthesize market research; create report	Outside consulting	March 2010

Determine areas for prototype development	Marketing and product development teams	April 2010
Design prototype	Product development team	May 2010
Conduct usability testing	Product development and marketing teams	July 2010

Your unit will need to determine *which people* within marketing or product development will be responsible for these specific tasks. The people to whom tasks in an action plan are delegated become the owners of those items.

If cross-functional teams have been created to carry out action plans, then they too will need to determine what their charter is, who will lead their effort, and how they will make decisions.

Gathering input from others

Establishing accountability can be challenging. How can you make sure all bases are covered? Get input from the owners of action plan tasks. Often, the people who are closest to the action can be particularly aware of the major and minor logistical concerns that a task may involve.

Consider getting input from people with varying levels of experience. Team members who have never handled a certain kind of project or task before may bring a helpful "beginner's mind" to the process—generating questions that a more seasoned person may not have considered. At the same time, an experienced employee may be able to offer additional valuable insights based on lessons learned from previous projects he or she has handled.

Tips for establishing accountability

- Decide who has responsibility for carrying out the tasks in your action plans.
- In establishing accountability for tasks, consider getting input from people who have never handled certain kinds of tasks before—as well as those who have extensive experience.
- Clarify how much autonomy people will have in carrying out their responsibilities. For example, do you prefer people to consult with you before making a decision? Or do you prefer that they decide and then inform you? Do you want them to obtain consensus from other team members before proceeding?
- To clarify autonomy, assess various team members' capabilities and preferences. Some people may feel more confident in their decisions if they can check out their thinking with you before making a choice. Others may have more experience with, and prefer, handling decisions by themselves. Still others may have little experience with "owning" decisions but lots of potential to excel in this area. Give this last group of people opportunities to make low-risk decisions themselves, to gain practice.
- Hold regular meetings with your task owners to help them both evaluate their successes and learn from their failures along the way. Discussing accomplishments and opportunities for improvement will help develop the skills of task owners.
- Ensure that the system you use for evaluating task owners is fair and equitable. Stars should be separated from nonperformers and rewarded accordingly.

Making judgment calls

Like many other managerial responsibilities, establishing accountability can involve complex judgment calls. Though this process may seem straightforward on the surface, you'll need to clarify how much autonomy people and teams will have in carrying out their responsibilities. For example:

- Do individuals need to consult others before making a decision?

- If so, for what types of decisions, and who needs to be consulted?

- Do you want team members to reach consensus before a decision is made?

Often, the answers to such questions will depend on your assessment of the various team members' capabilities and preferences. For instance:

- Some individuals may feel more confident in their decisions if they can check out their thinking with other team members before making a choice.

- Other team members might be interested in (and may have experience with) handling decisions by themselves.

- Still other individuals may have relatively little experience with "owning" decisions but lots of potential to excel in this area. You may want to give them the opportunity to make some lower-risk decisions themselves, without formal approval, to gain more practice.

Creating an
Environment
for Execution
Excellence

T eams become much more effective at executing strategy if their manager has created an environment for execution excellence. To foster such an environment, you'll need to help your employees adopt a strategic mind-set, instill the right values in the group's culture, develop your people's leadership skills, identify and address resistance to the execution of strategic plans, and train people for the future. We'll look at each of these below.

Developing a strategic mind-set in your group

To help your group excel at implementing strategic initiatives, cultivate a *strategic mind-set*—the shared belief that strategy is everyone's job. This means thinking strategically about the long term, and it requires a specific culture—a set of shared values and accepted behaviors. To instill the right values for a strategic mind-set in your group, you need to share the fundamentals of the strategy:

- Explain why the company's strategy is necessary. (Is it because of stiffening competition? Radical new technologies?)

- Explain how the initiatives that are being carried out support the corporate strategy. (Will they boost revenues? Enable the organization to enter new markets?)

- Outline what will happen if your group *succeeds* in implementing its plans. (Will the team win recognition and possible financial reward?)

- Outline what will happen if the group *fails* to implement its plans. (Will the company lose its competitive edge? Will some team members lose their jobs?)

- Finally, make clear what attitudes and behaviors are expected from each person on the team. (A willingness to work overtime, if necessary? To ask for help when needed?)

By regularly receiving such information, a group is more likely to adopt the shared belief that strategy truly is *everyone's* job.

Considering your culture

A group's culture influences what team members consider most important, how they resolve conflicts, and how they interact with each other. It also affects their choices about what they want or don't want to work on and the quality of their work. For example, a commonly held value such as customer orientation can guide employees in many situations to do the right thing that supports the company strategy—without the need for supervision.

All organizations have a culture—whether they've consciously cultivated it or not. And many organizations, especially larger ones, embark on culture-change programs in tandem with strategic change. So whether or not your unit has an established culture to guide it, you'll need to instill the right values for a strategic mind-set.

Fostering leadership

The best managers develop leadership abilities in their direct reports. That means identifying individuals who excel at any of the various capacities required by a unit—and putting these "stars" in key positions where they can advance the unit's strategic goals. In making such assignments, look for team members who exhibit qualities such as these:

- Integrity

- Visionary thinking

- Analytical and conceptual thinking

- Functional expertise

- Effective decision-making, interpersonal, and communication skills

- Drive and initiative

- Commitment to successful execution

By putting these individuals in roles related to executing strategy, you'll make the best use of their talents.

Identifying and addressing resistance

Like any form of change, strategic change is difficult, even painful, for many people. Thus, most managers encounter resistance from some direct reports when implementing a new initiative. Resistance might take many forms:

- Outright defiance

- Apparent agreement to do something, but failure to follow through

- An emotional attachment to the way things were previously done

- Diminishing commitment to the job

Whether these behaviors stem from ill intent or simply fear of the unknown, resistance to strategic initiatives can seriously impede your unit's efforts to execute strategy. Resisters not only threaten to slow efforts, but can also cost an organization a lot of money—and possibly even market share—by hampering strategic change.

Your unit can't do its part to support corporate strategy unless everyone shares an enthusiasm for the strategic initiatives. How should you deal with resisters? If an individual shows signs of balking at strategic change yet has valuable talents that you want to retain, consider these options:

- **Information:** Give the person plenty of information about the market forces that are forcing the company to change, how the company intends to deal with those forces, and what the corporate strategy and initiatives mean for that individual.

- **Involvement:** Invite the person to participate as much as possible in planning and executing initiatives, so he or she has a personal investment in the strategy and initiatives.

- **Coaching:** Identify reasons behind the resistance (fear of change? lack of information?) to see whether they can be overcome or corrected.

- **Performance improvement plan:** If necessary, with the help of your human resources group, develop a formal performance improvement plan whereby the individual is evaluated periodically against a set of defined objectives.

With resisters who can't be salvaged, you have little choice but to separate them from your unit as quickly as possible. Consider moving those people elsewhere—to areas in the organization where they may feel less resistant to change and therefore still be able to make a genuine contribution. If all else fails, consider dismissing them.

Training people for the future

Ongoing training is essential for enabling a unit to excel at executing strategy. Identify any new skills individuals will need in order to carry out new initiatives. These skills include using new analytic and decision-making tools, giving presentations, managing projects, and communicating with customers. Decide how and when the training will be provided.

Also consider training programs that deal specifically with strategic planning, project management, and change. Courses on topics such as where strategy comes from, how to interpret market forces, and why change is important can help individuals grasp the bigger picture and better understand their role in it.

A major strategic initiative provides an opportunity for everybody to develop management skills and to be a visible success within the company.

Evaluating
and Rewarding
Performance

With a strategic initiative well under way in your unit, one final process remains: evaluating the unit's performance and rewarding successful results. Through this process, you reinforce desired behaviors and attitudes—increasing the likelihood that your unit will perform even better while executing strategic efforts in the future.

Evaluating performance entails measuring how your unit has performed on its overall objectives, as well as how individuals have performed on their objectives. And it involves considering both quantitative and qualitative performance data as well as the types of rewards you'll use to foster additional success.

Using quantitative criteria

Most units have from four to six key result areas by which their success is typically measured. Different functions have different types of criteria. For example, a marketing group's performance might be measured by sales, market penetration, and distribution, while a manufacturing unit's performance might be measured by unit volume, cost, and quality.

Objectives that focus on revenue, cost of goods, market share, and so forth are quantifiable and measurable. For example, your unit might have an objective of increasing revenue by 10 percent annually over the next three years by putting several strategic initiatives into action. At the end of year 1, you'll review the revenue numbers and confirm whether revenue did in fact increase by 10 percent that year. If it did, that's a good sign that your group is executing strategy effectively.

Using qualitative criteria

Other criteria by which units and individuals are judged are less quantifiable and more qualitative. But these criteria are just as important. Specifically, as your group carries out strategic initiatives, watch for signs of the following forms of good performance:

- **Going the extra mile:** The unit *exceeds* expectations in its accomplishment of strategic initiatives.

- **Creativity:** Individuals are devising fresh and creative ways to accomplish the job—ways that could be used elsewhere in the organization.

- **Teamwork:** People are working together as a team—collaborating with one another, resolving conflicts, and sharing what they've learned.

- **Presentation skills:** Team members are able to get ideas across quickly to decision makers and move smoothly from discussions to action.

- **Planning:** People plan ahead and stay informed about what's coming—whether the news is good or bad.

- **Knowledge and learning:** Team members understand the company's business, their own role in supporting the corporate strategy, and the details of the action plans they're responsible for. They enthusiastically embrace learning new skills.

- **Attitudes and values:** Your people are demonstrating the attitudes and values required to achieve the unit's and company's strategic objectives.

Rewarding desired results

The question of how to compensate and otherwise reward people for good performance is a big subject, and different companies handle it in different ways. For instance, in some organizations, managers have extensive control over salaries, bonuses, stock options, and other forms of financial reward that may be offered to their direct reports. In other companies, top management determines the compensation system for the entire company, and managers have less say over how they reward their direct reports financially.

Often, reward and financial compensation systems are based on individual or group performance as measured by various specific criteria. Whatever reward system your company uses to reinforce excellence in strategy execution, it's important that employees understand how the system works. Specifically, answer the following questions for them:

- What exactly is expected of them, and what exactly will they receive if they perform well?

- Is the reward system permanent, or will it be modified or discontinued once strategic initiatives are fully implemented?

- Will everyone be eligible for rewards? For example, if the reward system features bonuses for sales of a new product, how will the product development people be rewarded for their contribution to the successful product?

Of course, most people value some form of financial reward for their work. Managers should find equitable ways to dole out pay raises, bonuses, stock options, and so forth to deserving individuals. But keep in mind that many people look for other kinds of reward from their work as well—which is helpful if financial rewards are limited. For example, people may value these rewards:

- **Recognition:** earning praise from peers and superiors; having the opportunity to show off an accomplishment or talk about a creative approach

- **Intellectual challenge:** working on mentally demanding projects

- **Power and influence:** making important decisions

- **Affiliation:** working with colleagues who share similar skills and interests

- **Managing people:** directing other people's efforts

- **Positioning:** gaining access to experience and contacts who will open doors to subsequent career moves

- **Lifestyle:** having the time to pursue other important interests in life (through such perks as flexible work schedules, work-share arrangements, and ample personal days)

- **Autonomy:** working with little supervision

- **Variety:** working on a mix of different projects

By combining financial and nonfinancial rewards—and tailoring them to individuals' unique preferences—you can foster an environment where your people strive for execution excellence again and again.

Tips and Tools

Tools for
Executing Strategy

Worksheet for Conducting a SWOT Analysis

Use a SWOT analysis to identify the strengths, weaknesses, opportunities, and threats relative to your company, unit or group, or a program you want to evaluate. The SWOT analysis lets you focus on specific areas and discover actions that can help build on strengths, minimize or eliminate weaknesses, maximize opportunities, and deal with or overcome threats.

Date of analysis:

What is being analyzed:

Internal Analysis

List factors inherent to what is being analyzed, such as the competencies of your group.

Strengths	Ideas for building on these strengths
Weaknesses	**Ideas for minimizing or repairing these weaknesses**

External Analysis

List factors external to what is being analyzed, such as customer needs or marketplace trends.

Opportunities	Ideas for investigating or taking advantage of these opportunities
Threats	**Ideas for minimizing or overcoming these threats**

Worksheet for Developing an Action Plan

Use this tool to develop an action plan for a strategic initiative that your group is implementing.

Program name:

Program manager:

Priority issue(s):

Objectives and metrics:

Resources:

Action Steps Required		
Task to be done	Person responsible	Due date

Interlocks Required		
Task to be done	Group/division/person responsible	Due date

Impact Estimate			
	Year 1	Year 2	Year 3
Revenue Sales:			
Gain Profit: Cost savings: Total:			
Cost Expense: Capital addition: Working-capital changes:			
Net results Cash flow: Present value: Profitability:			
People Number: Time required: Special skills:			

Worksheet for Determining Objectives from Key Result Areas

Use this tool to help you identify measures and objectives for each of your key result areas (KRAs). Remember that all of your objectives should be SMART—specific, measurable, achievable, realistic, and time-bound.

Key result area	Measures	Objectives
Example: cost	• Cost per unit • Units sold per employee per year	• Decrease cost per unit by 10 percent in 2004 • Increase units sold by 5 percent per employee by 2006

Alignment Checklist

Use this tool to check for misalignment between your action plan for a strategic initiative and the corporate strategy.

Part 1: Sources of Misalignment

For each statement below, check "Yes" if you think the statement accurately describes the implementation of your action plan. Check "No" if you think the statement doesn't accurately describe the implementation of your action plan.

Statement

As you began to implement your action plan, individuals added new objectives and new steps to the plan.

As you continued to implement the plan, people removed some objectives and steps to reduce costs or speed up implementation.

During implementation, you realized that you had left out certain tasks and needed to add them.

During implementation, the way certain tasks were handled didn't generate the desired results, and you realized you needed to change work processes.

During implementation, you discovered that your original estimates for time, effort, and costs required to carry out the plan's objectives were inaccurate.

If you checked "Yes" for any of the above statements, your plan may be off course or at risk of misalignment. However, that doesn't mean you should refuse to make any changes to your original plan. Instead, evaluate each proposed change in light of its relation to the corporate strategy and its impact on cost, schedule, team members' workloads, and so forth. Use part 2, below, to conduct this evaluation.

Part 2: Evaluating Proposed Changes

In the table below, list all the proposed changes to your action plan. For each change, fill in the potential implications.

Proposed change	Would the change support corporate strategy?	Change's impact on cost	Change's impact on schedule	Change's impact on resources

Creating an Environment-for-Excellence Checklist

Use this tool to assess how well you create an environment that encourages excellence.

Statement	Rating		
	All of the time	Some of the time	None of the time
I involve the members of my group in the strategic planning process.			
I explain to my group why the company's strategy is necessary and how our work supports that strategy.			
My group understands what will happen if it fails to implement our strategic initiatives.			
Members of my group understand what rewards (financial or otherwise) they will receive if they succeed in implementing our strategic initiatives.			
I take the time to identify any new skills that people will need to carry out our action plans, and I provide the necessary training.			
I clearly state the attitudes and behaviors I expect the members of my group to exhibit.			
The members of my group know exactly what they are allowed to do without consulting me—and what they must get my permission to do before acting.			
I identify individuals who excel in the capacities required by my group—and place them in key positions.			
I identify skeptics in my group, the reasons why they resist, and how any resistance can be overcome.			
I remove resistors whose behavior cannot be changed from my group.			

Ideas for Improvement
In light of your answers, what changes could you make to effectively cultivate an environment for excellence?

Test Yourself

This section offers ten multiple-choice questions to help you identify your baseline knowledge of the essentials of executing strategy. Answers to the questions are given at the end of the test.

1. What is a corporate strategy?

    a. A plan for clarifying who a company's customers are and what they value.

    b. A plan describing where a company wants to be and how it intends to get there.

    c. A plan spelling out your company's operational objectives for the next twelve months.

2. Which of the following best describes the components of a strategic plan?

    a. Direction statement, priority issues, strategic objectives, and action plans.

    b. Mission statement, the company's annual report, and analysis of industry trends.

    c. Vision statement, market position, and published statements to shareholders.

3. Which of the following is not a key component of an action plan?

    a. Required interlocks, or collaborations, between different departments.

    b. Metrics for measuring progress toward each objective.

    c. The rewards that will come with successful implementation of the plan.

4. If senior management has not delegated priority issues to your unit, how might you best identify your unit's priority issues?

    a. Brainstorm possible issues, and then evaluate whether they are realistic in light of your unit's available resources.

    b. Analyze external and internal factors, and then assess your unit's strengths, weaknesses, opportunities, and threats.

    c. Find out which interdepartmental collaborations might be necessary for your unit to support the corporate strategy.

5. Which of the following is the best example of a well-phrased strategic objective?

    a. "Have team members complete customer-service training."

    b. "Raise sales 10 percent annually over the next three years."

    c. "Provide better customer service than what all our rivals provide."

6. Your unit's action plans have just received approval from senior management. What is the best way to ensure that your action plans remain aligned with your company's strategy in the upcoming months?

a. Provide senior management monthly five- to six-page reports detailing what your unit has accomplished during the month, as well as performance reviews for each team member.

b. Provide senior management quarterly one- to two-page reviews that include what your unit has and has not accomplished during the past three months, as well as any key issues or other problems that need resolution.

c. Ask three to five members of your team to make a weekly presentation to senior management; the presentation should address what your unit has or has not accomplished, as well as any decisions that need to be made or resources that need to be allocated.

7. Once senior management has approved your unit's action plans and allocated the required resources, what do you do next?

a. Decide who will "own" the different tasks broadly defined in the plan.

b. Conduct a SWOT analysis to ensure that your action plan addresses all the company's strengths, weaknesses, opportunities, and threats.

c. Determine additional resources—including people, training, space, systems, and technology—necessary to carry out the action plan.

8. In implementing your unit's action plans, you've observed some resistance from a valued team member. How should you address the situation?

a. Separate the person from your group immediately to prevent damage to team morale—perhaps by moving the person to a position where he or she can contribute more willingly.

b. Provide the person with information about why the company's strategy is necessary, encourage participation in articulating and implementing the strategy, and use coaching to address the resistance.

c. Before actively addressing the situation, give the person adequate time to adapt and overcome any resistance.

9. You want to assess your group's implementation of a strategic initiative. In addition to evaluating the group's performance on objectively defined metrics (e.g., the number of potential new customers contacted this quarter), you need to consider other criteria as well. Which one of the following criteria would you not be likely to use?

a. Creativity—the group's ability to devise fresh ways of accomplishing a job.

b. Timeliness—whether the group has successfully accomplished its tasks within the time frame stated in the original plan.

c. Knowledge and learning—how deeply the team understands the company's business and the team's role in supporting the corporate strategy.

10. How can you best reward your team members for successfully implementing your company's strategy?

a. Emphasize the possibility of public recognition for all team members' accomplishments, including memos of praise to upper management.

b. Combine your available financial and nonfinancial rewards, and customize them according to each team member's reward values.

c. Make monetary compensation (whether it's raises, bonuses, or stock options) the centerpiece of your reward system.

Answers to test questions

1, b. A company's strategy consists of a plan for where it wants to go and how it intends to get there. Managers formulate strategy by asking fundamental questions such as these: Who are our customers, and what do they value? What products or services should we offer them? How will our customers and competitors change over time? How can we better position our company in our industry, given business trends? How can we distinguish ourselves from our rivals to remain competitive despite changes in our playing field?

2, a. A direction statement lays out the company's mission (purpose), vision (deeply desired future), business definition (offerings, customers, markets), competitive advantages, core competencies, and values. Examples of priority issues might include customer loyalty or service. Each priority issue may have several corresponding high-level strategic objectives—for example, "To increase customer loyalty, we need to boost repeat orders 20 percent and develop a loyalty program by year-end." A single priority issue many spawn two or three action plans—critical steps that must be taken to accomplish the priority issue at the unit level.

3, c. Interlocks and metrics *are* components of an action plan. Rewards for successful implementation of the plan are *not*, although managers should design a system for evaluating and rewarding successful implementation. Decisions about how to evaluate and reward performance are part of executing strategy, not components of an action plan.

4, b. By analyzing external and internal factors and then assessing your unit's strengths, weaknesses, opportunities, and threats (a SWOT analysis), you can identify priority issues that support the corporate strategy, play to your team's strengths, and enable your group to leverage important new opportunities and avert threats. Strengths and weaknesses stem from a group's *internal* characteristics. For instance, a team may excel at solving problems quickly, but may be less skilled at forging positive, long-term relationships with customers. Opportunities and threats generally come from *outside* a company. For example, a key supplier is offering steeper discounts (an opportunity) or raising prices drastically (a threat).

5, b. This objective is phrased in a way that meets the SMART criteria: it's specific, measurable, achievable, realistic, and time-bound. Objectives that are phrased in ways that don't meet these criteria are often vague or unrealistic, which makes them difficult for employees to understand and carry out. When you phrase objectives in SMART ways, you make it easier to translate the objectives into metrics for evaluating progress. For example, the goal "Raise sales 10 percent annually over the next three years" could be translated into the metric "percent increase in sales per year over the specified period."

6, b. Quarterly reviews are an efficient tool for assessing progress and checking alignment. Units should submit short reports for each of the action plans they are working on. These reports should address what the unit has accomplished, what the unit hasn't accomplished but said it would, which key issues need resolution, which decisions or resources the unit needs from senior management, and what the performance objectives are, if relevant.

7, a. Once corporate has allocated the necessary resources, your unit is ready to execute its action plans. The first step is to establish accountability for each of the tasks defined in each plan. Who will be responsible for what? Deciding exactly who should own each task can be challenging, but this step is critical to an effectively managed plan rollout. Since the people who are responsible for each of the tasks will be the closest to the action, they are the most likely to be aware of any logistical concerns or other issues that may develop as the plan is executed.

8, b. It's important to promptly address any resistance to your strategic plan. Otherwise, the plan may fail—often resulting in lost market share, decreased morale, and depleted company resources. Begin by providing information about the strategy, encouraging participation in its implementation, and coaching team members whom you value (and who you believe can overcome their own resistance). If these measures aren't successful, then it's best to separate such individuals from the group—perhaps by moving them to a different part of the organization where they can make a contribution more willingly.

9, b. If you've already evaluated objectively defined metrics, you've probably included timeliness, since it's an objective measure. In addition to objective accomplishments, managers also need to evaluate more *subjective* criteria for performance—such as creativity, knowledge and learning, teamwork, presentation skills, and ability to plan. These skills and attitudes play a crucial role in your team's ability to carry out your unit's action plans effectively. Without these qualities, no team can truly excel.

10, b. Though each company handles compensation differently, often the most effective reward systems offer both financial and nonfinancial rewards and are customized to meet individuals' preferences. In addition to raises, bonuses, or stock options, many people value forms of nonfinancial reward—such as flexible schedules, public recognition, opportunities to work on challenging assignments, and a chance to collaborate with colleagues they like. By getting to know what each team member values most in terms of nonfinancial rewards, you can customize a reward system that will inspire your group to even greater performance.

To Learn More

Articles

Gadiesh, Orit, and James L. Gilbert. "Transforming Corner-Office Strategy into Frontline Action." *Harvard Business Review*, OnPoint Enhanced Edition, May 2001.

In addition to a strategic plan and companywide meetings, organizations use other channels to communicate their strategy to managers and employees. Orit Gadiesh and James Gilbert call one of these channels a *strategic principle*—a memorable, action-oriented phrase that distills the company's strategy. Here are some examples: Southwest Airlines' "Meet customers' short-haul travel needs at fares competitive with the cost of automobile travel"; AOL's "Consumer connectivity first—anytime, anywhere"; eBay's "Focus on trading communities."

A good strategic principle encourages managers and employees to focus on the corporate strategy and take risks in identifying ways to support the strategy. By communicating your company's strategic principle frequently and consistently, you'll soon have people throughout your organization—as well as customers and competitors—"chanting the rant."

Kaplan, Robert S., and David P. Norton. "How to Implement a New Strategy Without Disrupting Your Organization." *Harvard Business Review*, March 2006.

Is structural change the right tool for the job? The answer is usually no, Robert Kaplan and David Norton contend. It's far less disruptive to choose an organizational design that works without major conflicts and then design a customized strategic system to align that structure to the strategy. A management system based on the balanced-scorecard (BSC) framework is the best way to align strategy and structure, the authors suggest. Managers can use the tools of the framework to drive their unit's performance: strategy maps to define and communicate the company's value proposition, and the scorecard to implement and monitor the strategy. In this article, the originators of the BSC describe how two hugely different organizations—DuPont and the Royal Canadian Mounted Police—used corporate scorecards and strategy maps organized around strategic themes to realize the enormous value that their portfolios of assets, people, and skills represented. As a result, the two organizations avoided a painful series of changes that would simply replace one rigid structure with another.

Norton, David P., and Randall H. Russell. "Translate the Strategy into Operational Terms." *Balanced Scorecard Report*, May 2005.

By now, the balanced scorecard's universal appeal as a management approach is well established. In its 2002 benchmarking data report, the Hackett Group found that 96 percent of the nearly two thousand global companies it surveyed had implemented, or planned to implement, the BSC. The real issue, though, isn't how many companies are using this approach, but, rather, whether they are using it properly. In the BSC's fifteen-year history, the core message has remained the same: to achieve breakthrough results, you must be able to manage strategy. And to manage strategy, you must first be able to describe it—translate it into a language that everyone understands.

Porter, Michael E. "What Is Strategy?" *Harvard Business Review*, OnPoint Enhanced Edition, February 2000.

Today's dynamic markets and technologies have called into question the sustainability of competitive advantage. Under pressure to improve productivity, quality, and speed, managers have embraced tools such as total quality management, benchmarking, and reengineering. Dramatic operational improvements have resulted, but rarely have these gains translated into sustainable profitability. And gradually, the tools have taken the place of strategy. As managers push to improve on all fronts, they move further away from viable competitive positions. Michael Porter argues that operational effectiveness, although necessary for superior performance, is not sufficient, because its techniques are easy to imitate. In contrast, the essence of strategy is choosing a unique and valuable position rooted in systems of activities that are much more difficult to match.

Van Zwieten, John. "How Not to Waste Your Investment in Strategy." *Training & Development*, June 1999.

In this article, John Van Zwieten explores six common dilemmas faced by executive and lower-level managers attempting to change strategic direction. He then provides a diagnosis for each dilemma and offers lessons. For example, one dilemma is characterized by divisions that are working at cross-purposes. Such companies, the author explains, are likely to encourage competition between divisions. The solution? An overarching vision of how divisions can cooperate, including a plan for presenting "one face" to customers.

Books

Fogg, C. Davis. *Implementing Your Strategic Plan: How to Turn "Intent" into Effective Action for Sustainable Change.* New York: AMACOM, 1999.

This book lays out the steps required to understand your company's strategy and strategic plan, develop a unit plan, and implement your unit plan. C. Davis Fogg organizes the book around eighteen keys to successful implementation of a plan. These include establishing accountability; turning strategic priorities into assigned, measurable action plans; fostering creative leadership and mental toughness; removing resistance; allocating resources effectively; empowering employees; and communicating strategy to everyone, all the time.

The book includes a wealth of examples, practical advice, and techniques for turning strategic plans into reality. Though aimed at senior managers, it offers lessons for other managers and team leaders at every level of an organization.

Fogg, C. Davis. *Team-Based Strategic Planning: A Complete Guide to Structuring, Facilitating, and Implementing the Process.* New York: AMACOM, 1994.

Fogg focuses on strategic planning in a team environment, exploring six key aspects: (1) structure and customization—designing the planning process to meet the needs of your organization, (2) facilitation—making things happen, from running meetings to documenting decisions, (3) teamwork—building teams and resolving conflicts, (4) leadership—forging the vision and making the plan operational, (5) organizational involvement—gaining commitment at all levels, and (6) information gathering and analysis—benchmarking, competitive analyses, and other valuable techniques.

Examples from actual companies illustrate each step of the process, and case studies reveal what worked and what didn't. The book also includes hands-on tools for mastering the strategic planning process.

Markides, Constantinos C. *All the Right Moves: A Guide to Crafting Breakthrough Strategy.* Boston: Harvard Business School Press, 2000.

Constantinos Markides explores the key questions companies must answer to define a strategy: Whom should we target as customers? What products or services should we offer them? How should we do this efficiently? How can we differentiate ourselves from rivals to stake out a unique competitive position?

But even the best strategies have a limited life. Companies must continually create new strategic positions—often by breaking the rules of the game. *All the Right Moves* reveals how creative thinking—including examining an issue from a variety of angles and experimenting with new ideas—leads to strategic innovation.

Strategy formulation also requires companies to make tough choices. This book offers concrete advice for thinking through those choices—systematically and successfully.

eLearning Programs

Harvard Business School Publishing. *Case in Point*. Boston: Harvard Business School Publishing, 2004.

Case in Point is a flexible set of online cases designed to help prepare middle- and senior-level managers for a variety of leadership challenges. These short, reality-based scenarios provide sophisticated content to create a focused view into the realities of the life of a leader. Your managers will experience realistic challenges under the following case headings: Aligning Strategy, Removing Implementation Barriers, Overseeing Change, Anticipating Risk, Ethical Decisions, Building a Business Case, Cultivating Customer Loyalty, Emotional Intelligence, Developing a Global Perspective, Fostering Innovation, Defining Problems, Selecting Solutions, Managing Difficult Interactions, The Coach's Role, Delegating for Growth, Managing Creativity, Influencing

Others, Managing Performance, Providing Feedback, and Retaining Talent.

Harvard Business School Publishing. *Managing Change.* Boston: Harvard Business School Publishing, 2000.

According to leadership experts, 70 percent of all corporate initiatives for change fail. This interactive program combines the theory and research of five change strategists to quickly and easily help managers balance pace and roll out change initiatives successfully. Managers will learn the numerous phases of change, critical mistakes to avoid, how to initiate carefully paced periods of smaller change, and how to lead successfully through change. Lessons include how to balance content, processes, and employees' emotions during a change initiative; how to maintain continuous change without tearing the organization apart (dynamic stability); how to navigate the phases of a change; and how to utilize empowered employees and trust to support a change effort.

Harvard Business School Publishing. *What Is a Leader?* Boston: Harvard Business School Publishing, 2001.

This interactive program helps managers apply concepts and grow from a competent manager to an exceptional leader. Use this program to assess your ability to lead your organization through fundamental change, to evaluate your leadership skills by examining how you allocate your time, and to analyze your "emotional intelligence" to determine your strengths and weaknesses as a leader. In addition, work through interactive, realistic scenarios to determine what approach to take when diagnosing problems and to learn how to manage and even use the stress associated with change, how to empower others, and how to practice empathy when managing the human side of interactions. Based on the research and writings of John Kotter, author of *Leading Change*, and other top leadership experts of today, this program is essential study for anyone charged with setting the direction of—and providing the motivation for—a modern organization.

Sources for Executing Strategy

The following sources aided in development of this book:

Butler, Timothy, and James Waldroop. *Discovering Your Career in Business*. New York: Perseus Books, 1997.

C. Davis Fogg Management Consulting, Inc. *Departmental Planning Process Guide*. Wakefield, RI: C. Davis Fogg Management Consulting, 1997.

Fogg, C. Davis. *Implementing Your Strategic Plan: How to Turn "Intent" into Effective Action for Sustainable Change*. New York: AMACOM, 1999.

———. *Team-Based Strategic Planning: A Complete Guide to Structuring, Facilitating and Implementing the Process*. New York: AMACOM, 1994.

Gadiesh, Orit, and James L. Gilbert. "Transforming Corner-Office Strategy into Frontline Action." *Harvard Business Review*, OnPoint Enhanced Edition, May 2001.

Johnson, Lauren Keller. "Helping New Managers Make the Leap to Leadership: An Interview with Linda A. Hill." *Harvard Management Update*, September 2003.

Levine, Harvey A. "Managing the Baseline and Controlling Creep." Parts 2 and 3. MyPlanView.com. Accessed July 22, 2003.

Porter, Michael E. "What Is Strategy?" *Harvard Business Review*, OnPoint Enhanced Edition, November–December 1996.

Notes

Notes

Notes

Notes

Notes

Notes

Notes

Notes

Notes

Notes